BASSOON

4606

3

4606

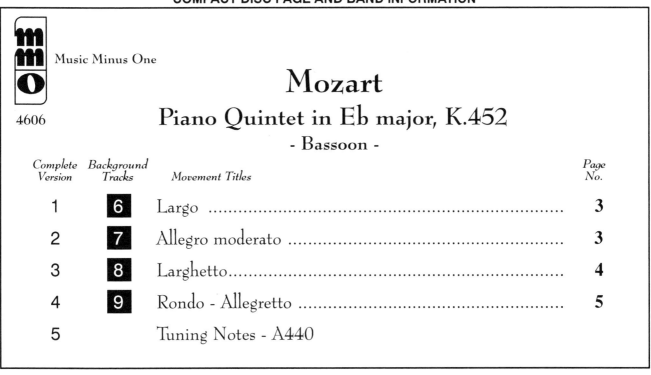

Music Minus One

4606

Mozart
Piano Quintet in Eb major, K.452
- Bassoon -

Complete Version	Background Tracks	Movement Titles	Page No.
1	6	Largo	3
2	7	Allegro moderato	3
3	8	Larghetto...	4
4	9	Rondo - Allegretto	5
5		Tuning Notes - A440	

Music Minus One • 50 Executive Boulevard • Elmsford, New York 10523-1325
Website: www.musicminusone.com   Phone: 914-592-1188 • Fax: 914-592-3575

Music Minus One Bassoon

4606

Mozart

Piano Quintet in Eb Major, K.452

Music Minus One • 50 Executive Boulevard • Elmsford, New York 10523-1325
Website: www.musicminusone.com   Phone: 914-592-1188 • Fax: 914-592-3575